AF372183

Look What I Got

This book belongs to: ______________

C-DER™
CHEETAH Decodable & Early Readers

Dear CHEETAH® family:

Our little books were specifically created to help our early readers master their decoding skills and build reading fluency. The repetitive use of high-frequency words, word families, decodable words, rhymes, and vivid illustrations facilitates this process. Our stories complement the objectives and content highlighted in the Jamaica Early Childhood Curriculum Guide and the Ministry of Education and the Grade 1 National Standards Curriculum of the Ministry of Education and Youth.

In journeying through our series, our little ones will develop a deeper awareness of and appreciation for our Jamaican culture. Our books also have universal appeal, as any early reader can identify with the characters, events and subjects in our texts. Readers will get enjoy the stories, build vocabulary, and exercise critical thinking by engaging in the activities at the end of each story.

Additionally, as a precursor to our series, or as a support to it, we've created a decodable 'sentence strip' book for the very young readers and those who require more scaffolding.

Happy reading!

CHEETAH®

Chasing and capturing your dreams with you.

The more you explore, the more you'll discover. Let's go on an adventure and learn!

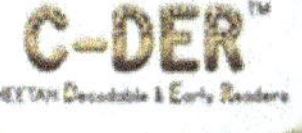

My decodable words:

**bow, grow, know, low,
mow, row, sow, slow, tow**

Letter sounds:

- long vowel sound /ō / as in digraphs 'oa' and 'ow' in the medial and final positions in words

- long vowel sound /ō/ as in 'VCC' pattern

Word families: 'ow'

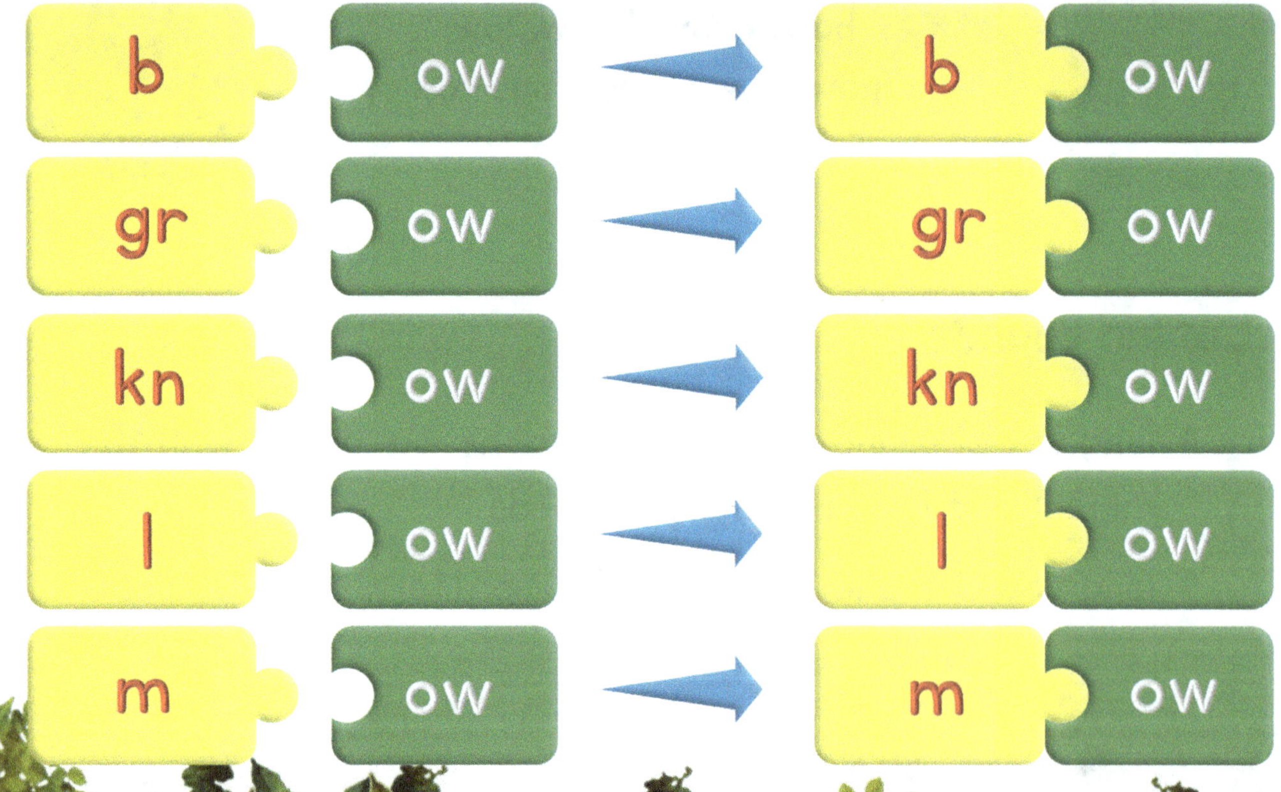

C-DER
CHEETAH Decodable & Early Readers
1

Look What I Got

'Look what I got as gifts!' Ken says.

'I got lots of things. I can have fun for days!

I got a toy can to water the plants in a row,

so the seeds that we sow can grow and grow!

C-DER
CHEETAH Decodable & Early Readers
3

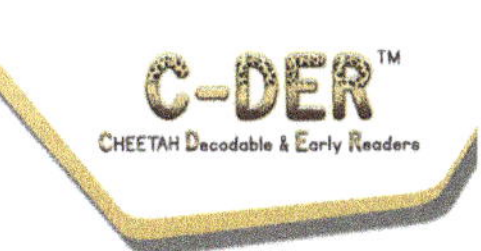

Do you know the name of a truck that can tow?

Yes, a tow truck! Mine came in a bag with a bow.

Now I can tow my cars when they stall,

and I can carry trees when they fall.

5

Mom and Dad know that I like the water a lot,

so they got me a boat. I just love my new yacht!

I can make it go fast or make it go slow.

My yacht can also race, you know!

C-DER™
CHEETAH Decodable & Early Readers
7

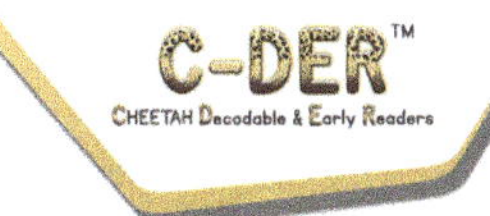

I like to help Daddy
to cut the grass,

so that it can look pretty
to people who pass.

Now, I have my own tool,
so I can mow,

and the grass won't get
tall; it will be kept low.

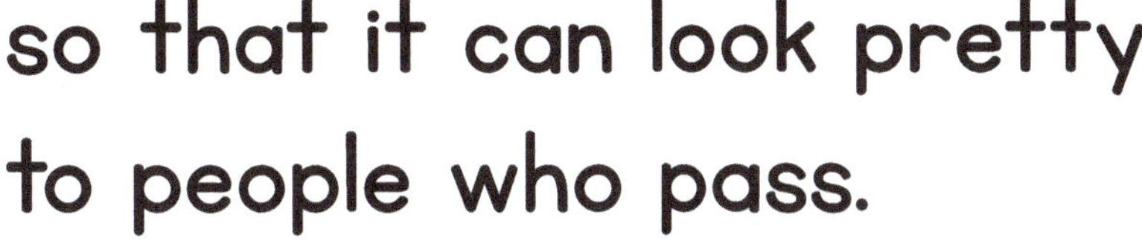

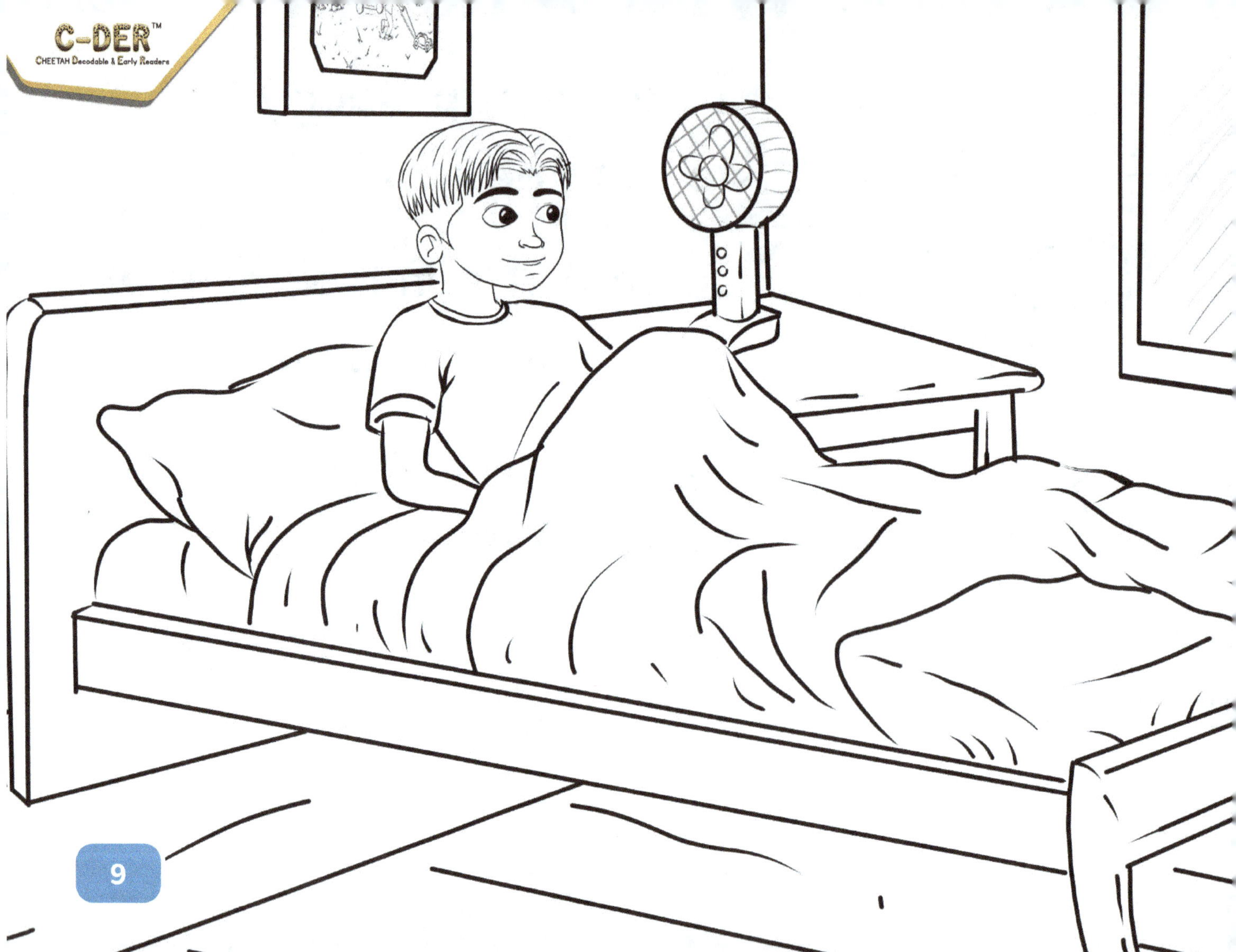
C-DER
CHEETAH Decodable & Early Readers
9

I really like my new little fan.

Now, I can keep as cool as I can.

I can sleep better at night when it is hot.

The cool air from my fan helps me a lot.

C-DER
CHEETAH Decodable & Early Readers
11

My kite is so cool! It can fly up high.

I love how my kite can dance in the sky.

I go out in the yard on a windy day,

and I let the wind take it up, up and away!

C-DER
CHEETAH Decodable & Early Readers

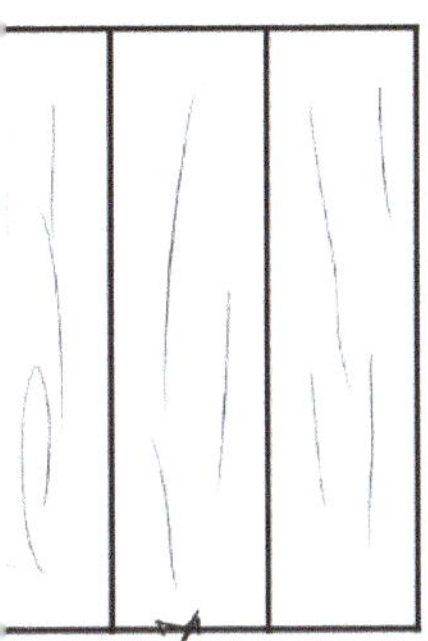

Take a look at my new red coat.

Mom gave me this one with a little note.

It said, "This will warm you when it is cold."

It looks nice! It is very bright and bold.

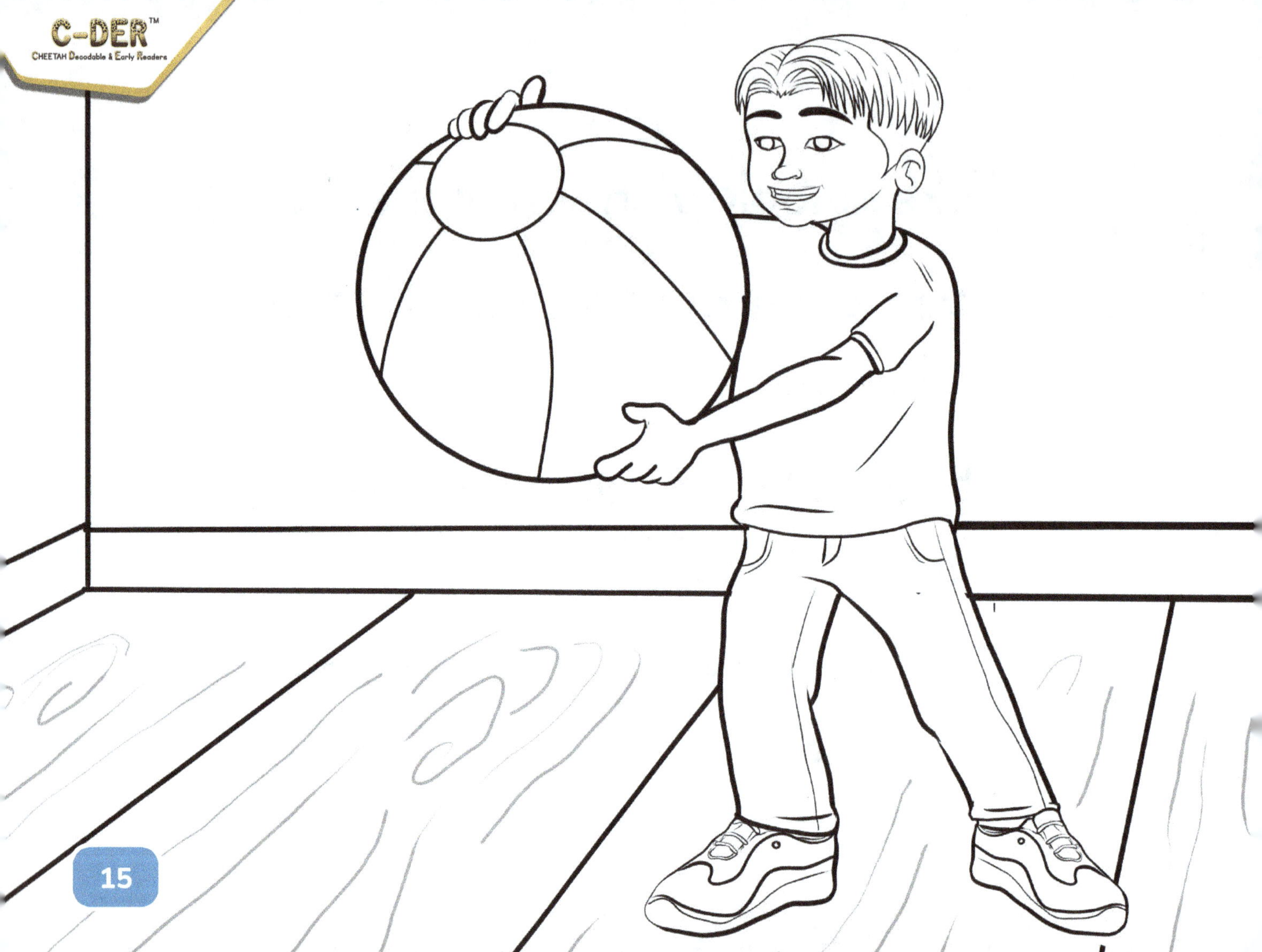

C-DER™
CHEETAH Decodable & Early Readers
15

Of all my gifts, I love this one best;

I love my new ball more than all the rest.

I can do many things with my ball.

That is why I love it best of all.'

Discussion and activities:

1. Have the children talk about different gifts they have received and the different occasions they got these gifts.

2. Have the children identify the words with the target letter and sound.

3. Have the children make the sound of the target letter and identify rhyming words in the text.

Discussion and activities:

4. Discuss the words *yacht, stall, tow,* and *bold* as used in the context of the story.

5. Have the children read the text aloud.

6. Have the children colour the images.

Questions:

1. What is the tool that Ben got so that he can mow the grass?

....

2. What sort of things do you think Ben can do with his ball?

....